A RIVER JOURNEY
The Mississippi

Simon Milligan & Martin Curtis

A RIVER JOURNEY

The Amazon   The Ganges
The Mississippi   The Nile
The Rhine   The Yangtze

For more information on this series and other Hodder Wayland titles, go to
www.hodderwayland.co.uk

A River Journey: *The Mississippi*

Commissioning Editor: Victoria Brooker
Book Editor: Belinda Hollyer
Book consultant: John Gerrard
Series consultant: Rob Bowden

Designer: Jane Hawkins
Picture Research: Shelley Noronha, Glass Onion Pictures
Maps: Tony Fleetwood
Cover Design: Hodder Wayland

Series concept by: Environment and Society International –
Educational Resourcing

British Library Cataloguing in Publication Data
Milligan, Simon
   Mississippi. - (A river journey)
   1. Mississippi River - Juvenile literature
   2. Mississippi River - Geography - Juvenile literature
   I. Title II Curtis, Martin
   917.7
ISBN 0750240342

Printed in China
Hodder Children's Books
A division of Hodder Headline Limited
338 Euston Road, London NW1 3BH

The website addresses (URLs) included in this book were valid at the time of going to press. However, because of the nature of the Internet, it is possible that some addresses may have changed, or sites may have changed or closed down since publication. While the authors and Publisher regret any inconvenience this may cause readers, no responsibility for any such changes can be accepted by either the authors or the Publisher.

Picture Acknowledgements
Cover Peter Kingsford/Eye Ubiquitous; title page Eye Ubiquitous/L. Fordyce;
6 Eye Ubiquitous/L. Fordyce; 7 ZEFA; 8 Corbis; 9 Oxford Scientific Films/Norbert Rosing;
10 top Skyscan, bottom Topham; 11 left Oxford Scientific Films/Lon E. Lauber, right Oxford
Scientific Films/Alan and Sandy Carey; 12 Eye Ubiquitous/L. Fordyce; 13 Corbis; 14 Photri;
15 inset Photri; main Eye Ubiquitous/L. Fordyce; 16-17 Ecoscene/Andrew Brown, inset left
Zuma, inset right Peter Newark; 18 Topham; 19 Mary Evans Picture Library; 20 Skyscan;
21 Popperfoto/E. Garcia; 22 Eye Ubiquitous/L. Fordyce, inset AKG;
23 Photri; 24 AKG; 24 Photri, inset Topham; 26-27 Eye Ubiquitous/
L. Fordyce, inset Still Pictures; 28 Eye Ubiquitous/L. Fordyce;
29 Hulton; 30 Photri, inset Still Pictures; 32 James Davis;
33 PictorialPress, top Corbis; 34 Mary Evans, inset Still Pictures;
35 Camera Press;36 Hulton; 37 Topham; 38-39 Eye Ubiquitous/L. Fordyce,
inset Photri; 40 Oxford Scientific Films/C. C. Lockwood;
41 Ecoscene, top inset Oxford Scientific Films/C. C. Lockwood,
bottom inset Still Pictures/Nicole Duplaix; 42 Photri;
bottom Pictorial Press; 43 Robert Harding/Charles Bowman;
44-45 Oxford Scientific Films/ C. C. Lockwood,
bottom Oxford Scientific Films/Jack Dermid.

The maps in this book use a conical projection,
and so the indicator for North on the main map
is only approximate.

Contents

SOURCE

NORTH DAKOTA

CANADA

LAKE SUPERIOR

Red Lake

1

Lake Itasca

MINNESOTA

MICHIGAN

St. Paul

MINNEAPOLIS

2

WISCONSIN

SOUTH DAKOTA

Minnesota River

LAKE MICHIGAN

MICHIGAN

Missouri River

IOWA

CHICAGO

NEBRASKA

Moline

INDIANA

Illinois River

ILLINOIS

3

Hannibal

Ohio River

ST. LOUIS

KANSAS

Kaskaskia River

MISSOURI

KENTUCKY

4

APPALACHIAN MOUNTAINS

TENNESSEE

Arkansas River

OKLAHOMA

MEMPHIS

Tennessee River

ARKANSAS

Ouachita River

Tombigbee River

MISSISSIPPI

ALABAMA

Alabama River

Apalachicola River

LOUISIANA

5

Red River

TEXAS

Atchafalaya River

Baton Rouge

NEW ORLEANS

GULF OF MEXICO

MOUTH

mountain ranges

N

drainage basin

kilometres
0   100   200

miles
0   25   50   75   100   125   150

Atlantic
Ocean

Pacific
Ocean

Your Guide to the River

USING THEMED TEXT As you make your journey down the Mississippi you will find topic headings about that area of the river. These symbols show what the text is about.

NATURE   Plants, wildlife and the environment

HISTORY   Events and people in the past

PEOPLE   The lives and culture of local people

CHANGE   Things that have altered the area

$ ECONOMY   Jobs and industry in the area

USING MAP REFERENCES   Each chapter has a map that shows the section of the river we are visiting. The numbered boxes show exactly where a place of interest is located.

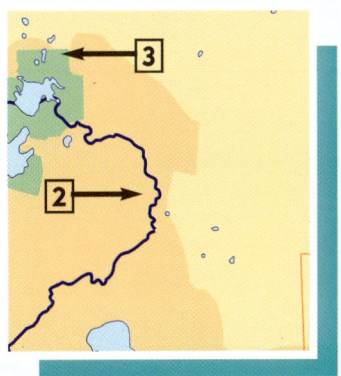

The Journey Ahead

From Lake Itasca, a small clear stream slowly starts its winding journey southwards. As we travel down the upper river from Minneapolis and St Paul, we pass through thirty locks and dams. These were built to help navigation. This stretch of the Mississippi employs nearly 50,000 people in the barge industry.

Next, we pass through the state of Iowa, America's leading producer of corn, soybeans, and pigs. It has some of the most fertile agricultural land in the world. Near the city of St Louis, we can see where the river broke its banks in 1993, flooding an enormous area.

Further downstream the Mississippi is more than 1,000 metres wide, because the Missouri, the Ohio and the Tennessee rivers add to the volume of water. In the meandering lower river we pass through an earthquake zone and visit Memphis, the home of Blues music.

An ocean-going tanker meets us at Baton Rouge, and takes us through the wide delta. Finally, after a journey of 3,780 kilometres, the Mississippi spills into the Gulf of Mexico, on the coast of the state of Louisiana.

So grab your paddle and jump in the canoe as we start our journey from Lake Itasca, the source of the mighty Mississippi.

1. The Head Waters

THIS FIRST SECTION OF THE RIVER is 672 kilometres long. It takes us through a state park and a Native American reservation. It's easy to paddle the canoe here, because the descent is gentle and the water flows slowly. The lakes, forests and marshlands we pass all provide a rich habitat for plants and wildlife. Look out for eagles, racoons, and maybe even a black bear as we paddle downstream. There are some rapids ahead, so make sure you have your buoyancy aid and helmet on.

Below: Lake Itasca, in the state of Minnesota. You can see how shallow the water is here, where the Mississippi River begins.

NATURE *Looking for the source*

Native Americans have used the Mississippi for many centuries. The first European to see the river was the Spanish explorer, Hernando de Soto, in the sixteenth century. In 1832, an American explorer called Henry Schoolcraft claimed that Lake Itasca was the Mississippi's source. This is still thought to be true. But Elk Lake, and a small stream called Nicollet Creek, both feed into Lake Itasca - and so one of these might be the true source.

Further downstream the mighty river is often more than 1,000 metres wide, but it trickles from Lake Itasca as a stream just four metres wide and less than a half a metre deep. It is from here that our adventure begins.

HISTORY *The great freeze*

The history of the Mississippi River is more than a million years old, but the headwaters and upper Mississippi were only shaped in the last Ice Age. During that 'great freeze' about 10,000 years ago, vast ice sheets reached the area that is now the states of Minnesota, Wisconsin, Iowa and Illinois.

Glacial lakes were formed when the climate grew warmer. The ice sheets (which may have been up to 3,000 metres thick) retreated north. Meltwater carrying gravel, sand and clay wove through ridges of deposited material, creating deep channels. Today, these channels are still followed by the upper Mississippi and the streams that

Above: Thick forests of pine and birch trees, like these, line this section of the Upper Mississippi.

join it. The Ice Age created perfect conditions for the forests of pine, oak, maple, birch and aspen to flourish, after the ice sheets melted.

Lake Itasca is just one of more than a hundred glacial lakes in the Itasca State Park. **MAP REF: 1** The Park was established in 1891 to protect the natural pine forests from the logging industry. About 500,000 people now visit the park each year for camping, hiking, fishing and water sports.

Above: A detail of traditional Ojibwe dress.
Left: These Ojibwe men are harvesting wild rice in the Leech Lake Reservation, at the river's edge.

✋ PEOPLE *The Ojibwe*

Long before European settlers first arrived, the Ojibwe made the Mississippi their home. The Ojibwe are Native Americans. For centuries, they fished the Mississippi, built birch bark canoes to sail on it, farmed its floodplains, and harvested wild rice from its banks. In the nineteenth century the Leech Lake Reservation MAP REF: 2 was formed. Many Ojibwe people still live in this area of the state of Minnesota.

The Ojibwe were once one of the most powerful Native American nations. Today, with over 100,000 people, they are the third largest group of Native Americans in the United States. Some Ojibwe still fish and farm in traditional ways on the Leech Lake Reservation. Others have built casinos, and tourist businesses. But most of the land on the Reservation is not owned by the Ojibwe. Their leaders are worried that the land may be taken away from them in the future.

NATURE *Busy beavers*

Beavers are the largest rodent in the United States. They are just one of fifty-seven species of mammal that inhabit this stretch of the Mississippi. Beavers can cut down trees with their large teeth. As we paddle along the gently flowing water between Lake Itasca and Lake Cass, we can see the dams they have built from mud, sticks, and logs. The dams create ponds of still water where the beavers construct their homes, called lodges.

HISTORY *Fur trading*

The Mississippi played a big role in America's fur trapping and trading industry.

French and British companies fought for control of the fur trade throughout the eighteenth century, and the riverside settlement of St Cloud in Minneapolis became very important. Tens of thousands of beavers were trapped and killed to supply fur to European markets, and millions of dollars-worth of beaver fur was shipped along the Mississippi. In the nineteenth century beaver numbers fell dramatically, and when fashions changed the fur trade became less important. Today, trapping is strictly regulated.

Below: A beaver tucking fresh willow branches into the walls of its lodge.

✋ PEOPLE *Fun on the water*

People from Minnesota State are water lovers, and they use the Mississippi and the 12,000 surrounding lakes for year-round activities. There are more boats per person in Minnesota than in any other American state. Water-skiing was invented here on Lake Pepin MAP REF: 3 in 1922.

If you enjoy fishing, we can catch walleye, trout, or bass at one of the resorts between the towns of Bemidji and Grand Rapids. People even continue fishing in the cold of winter. They build heated 'fish houses' on the frozen lakes, and cut holes through the ice floor for their fishing lines.

There's also cross-country skiing, ice-skating and ice hockey in winter-time.

Top: Lake Minnetonka is the largest lake in Minnesota's Hennepin County.
Above: Ice fishers celebrating a catch. You can rent fish houses by the day, and many lake towns hold ice-fishing competitions.

If you prefer hot weather, you can cycle and swim in the summer. But make sure you pack insect repellent, because mosquitoes can be a problem here!

Left: A logger at work. This process, of cutting a fallen tree into smaller lengths, is called bucking. Above: There are about 2,000 timber wolves in Minnesota - the largest population outside Alaska.

$ ECONOMY *Forestry & logging*

Logging has always been an important part of Minnesota's economy, and the Mississippi played a central role in transporting lumber downstream. Massive conifer forests were cleared in the nineteenth and early twentieth centuries. Trees were cut in winter, and stacked beside streams. When the snow melted in spring, the loggers launched the logs into the water and floated them downstream to the Mississippi River, and then on to the city of Minneapolis.

Production reached its peak in 1905, but Minnesota's logging industry stills employs about 60,000 people. Trees such as aspen are cut to make paper, and hardwoods like oak and maple are felled to make furniture.

More than thirty per cent of the land in Minnesota was still forested in 1993, but environmental campaigners are worried about the impacts of the industry. Logging rates have tripled since 1975. If this continues, an area greater than 365 football fields will soon be cleared of forest every day. This would destroy natural habitats, and endanger timber wolves and lynx.

📖 HISTORY *The Great River Road*

As we approach the sprawling cities of St Paul and Minneapolis, we can see the Great River Road. The road is 4,800 kilometres long, and runs the entire length of the river, following the route of the early explorers. Visitor centres and museums along the road tell the story of the Mighty Mississippi.

Do you have your map handy? If so, let's jump on board a giant tow and navigate the locks and dams of the upper river!

St. Paul

MINNEAPOLIS

km 0 — 100
miles 0 — 50

1

WISCONSIN

IOWA

Moline

ILLINOIS

Illinois River

Hannibal

Kaskaskia River

2 ST. LOUIS

2. The Upper Section

FROM THE WILDERNESS OF THE MARSHLANDS, the wooded shores, and the gentle rapids of the headwaters, we emerge into a wide river valley. Here, spectacular bluffs rise more than fifty metres on either side of the Mississippi. Large, bustling cities and vast agricultural lands await us as we travel through the heartlands of the central United States.

Below: The Upper Dam of St Anthony's Falls, with the city of Minneapolis behind them. You can see the Falls even more clearly in the old photograph on the opposite page.

PILLSBURY A MILL, LARGEST FLOUR MILL IN THE WORLD.
35,000
INTERNATIONAL STOCK FOOD FACTORY

Above: The Falls rush past an advertisement for Pillsbury's 'A' Flour Mill, in a 1912 photograph. The ruins of the 'A' mill can still be visited today.

NATURE The Falls of St Anthony

The Falls of St Anthony [MAP REF: 1] at the city of Minneapolis are a wonderful example of a 'retreating waterfall'. Waterfalls are created when water wears away soft rock more quickly than layers of hard rock. In time a small step develops, and the river falls over this into a large plunge pool below. When the soft rock is removed, the hard rock above is left unsupported. It falls into the river, making the waterfall move backwards.

Thirteen thousand years ago, the Falls were located twenty-two kilometres downstream, at the city of St Paul. As the soft rock was worn away, the waterfall moved upriver by about one metre every year. The waterfall once had very rough edges, but engineers smoothed these out with cement. Then they used the power of the falling water to generate electricity.

HISTORY Forests & flour

The 'Twin Cities' of Minneapolis and St Paul are separated by the Mississippi, and the river is the key to their prosperity. In 1819, the United States Army built Fort Snelling at the confluence of the Mississippi and Minnesota rivers, where Minneapolis is today. Fort Snelling protected the area and safeguarded river traffic. To supply the fort with timber, soldiers constructed a sawmill at the Falls of St Anthony - the only waterfall on the Mississippi. The energy of the falling water was used to saw logs, that were transported downstream from forests in the north.

The same energy was also used to power local flourmills. By 1870, only fifteen years after the settlement was founded, Minneapolis was the flour-milling capital of the world. The city grew rapidly as boats brought goods, tourists, and settlers to the area. Today only three flourmills remain, and none uses water power. The Twin Cities have now become successful manufacturing centres, and support a population of over two and a half million people.

Pig's Eye

The city of St Paul was originally called Pig's Eye. That's a strange name for a settlement that would become the state capital of Minnesota, in 1849. Pig's Eye began life in the 1830s, and was named after a retired fur trapper called Pierre 'Pig's Eye' Parrant.

Pig's Eye was well known to many Native Americans, soldiers, and river men, to whom he sold whisky! But an army commander insisted that the small cluster of businesses and residents settled around him should move further away to Fountain Cave (now part of downtown St Paul). This was the most northern point on the Mississippi that large cargo boats could navigate, and so Fountain Cave became an important port. It attracted many fur trappers, Native Americans, former soldiers, and others searching for work.

The city has grown dramatically since it was renamed St Paul in 1841, but its colourful history is still remembered. You can still see Pig's Eye Island in the river.

CHANGE *Stairway of water*

By the early twentieth century, logging had reduced the region's forests. The need for shipping on the Upper Mississippi had declined. At the same time, railroads struggled to serve the expanding industry and agriculture, and the growing number of people living in the region.

The Mississippi region had to take up this transport challenge, but engineers faced a significant problem. The river channel in the upper reaches was too

Below: The Upper Harbor Lock in St Paul, the northernmost point of commercial navigation along the Mississippi. The yellow bumpers help to guide river craft into the lock channel.

shallow to handle the new, large tows operating in the south. Transferring goods to smaller boats was too costly. Many people feared that without drastic action the region's economy would suffer.

The answer? The government constructed a series of dams and locks to create a three-metre-deep navigation channel. These changes allowed large river vessels to travel up and down the river. As navigation improved, the volume of goods carried on the Mississippi rose sharply. Today, river traffic is controlled by a series of thirty locks and dams between Minneapolis and Granite City. The Mississippi has become one of the busiest cargo routes in the United States.

Tows transport about eighty million tonnes of grain, petroleum products, coal, machinery and other goods every year. It would need 870 trucks to carry as much as just one tow! 'Towboaters' work in six-hour shifts for twenty-eight days, without a day off. The crew must eat, sleep, and shower onboard, because the tows travel day and night, without stopping.

Below (inset): A tow enters lock 19, at Keokuk in the state of Iowa.
Below: Towboats pushing groups of barges down the river, near Cairo. Just one barge can carry as much as 1,500 tonnes of cargo.

NATURE *Sea of grass*

The North American prairies cover a vast area in the central United States. They stretch from the Rocky Mountains in the west to the Mississippi in the east, and from the Canadian border in the north to the Mexican border in the south. The word 'prairie' comes from the French, and it was used by French trappers and explorers to describe the 'sea of grass' they found here.

Flat or hilly grasslands dominate the prairies. The grasses die down in autumn but return in the spring as the temperature rises and snowmelt and rain increase. Fires, caused by lightning and cattle-farmers trying to encourage grass growth, have kept forests to a minimum.

Below: This is what the tall prairie grasses look like. You can see Prairie Blazing Star (pink) and Black-eyed Susan (yellow) flowers blooming amongst the grasses.

In the seventeenth century, grizzly bears, wolves, prairie dogs, and tens of millions of bison and antelope, roamed the grasslands. Today, the environment is very different. As settlers advanced during the nineteenth century, displacing Native Americans, the use of the prairies changed dramatically. In place of small-scale hunting of bison with fires and traps, large numbers were killed with rifles. Cattle ranches and cereal farming became common. Wetlands have been drained for crop cultivation, rivers dammed, and larger areas given over to cereals such as wheat and maize. The very existence of the traditional tall prairie grasses has fallen sharply, and now less than 0.1% of Iowa's native prairies remain.

HISTORY *Deere & Company*

Prairie grasses form a very closely-knit sod. The native prairie grasses have very long roots that help to bind the soil together, and pioneer farmers found ploughing with wooden and iron tools very difficult.

John Deere, a young blacksmith and inventor, settled in Illinois in 1837 and within three years he and his partner had produced a new steel plough that could cope with the heavy, sticky soils. They were so successful that by 1855, their business was making about thirteen thousand ploughs a year! With Deere's invention, breaking the sod for cultivation became possible, and cereal farming thrived.

Nearly 150 years later, Deere & Company are still located at Moline, on the Mississippi River. The business is now a major international manufacturer of a wide range of farm machinery.

$ ECONOMY *Protecting the prairies*

Modern farming techniques and agricultural equipment have had a large impact on the local environment. With the discovery of the rich, fertile soil that lies beneath the prairie grass, this region became the 'food basket' of the United States. In 1997, Iowa produced more maize, soybeans and pigs than any other state in the country.

But the removal of the prairie grasses has exposed the soil to erosion by rain and wind. This is not only a serious environmental problem, but it has also led to lower crop yields. Farmers are losing tens, perhaps hundreds of millions of dollars each year, despite attempts to prevent erosion - such as planting trees, so the roots can help bind the soil together.

Right: The original John Deere plough.
Below: John Deere tractors today. You can see how far the technology has come!

$ ECONOMY *Illinois Waterway*

At the town of Grafton, in Illinois State, we can see the mouth of the Illinois Waterway. MAP REF: 2 This is an important access route from the Mississippi River to the town of Chicago, and to Lake Michigan. The Waterway opened in 1933, and is 541 kilometres long. It allows barges to transport cargoes of coal, petroleum, grain and other products from the Great Lakes in the north, to the Gulf of Mexico in the south. The Waterway is a combination of natural channels, such as the Lower Des Plaines River and the Illinois River, and an artificial channel called the Chicago Sanitary and Ship Canal.

Above: A tug enters the Illinois Waterway in Chicago. You can see the bridges ahead are all rising, to let tall water traffic pass along the system.

PEOPLE *Mark Twain*

Nearly 200 kilometres downstream from the Waterway, we reach the small town of Hannibal. It has a population of only 20,000 people, and yet many tourists flock to the area.

Why? Because of a young man called Samuel Clemens, who lived in the town between 1839 and 1853. Samuel Clemens is better known as Mark Twain, the author of novels and stories about the Mississippi River. In *The Adventures of Huckleberry Finn*, Twain tells the story of a boy called Huck who flees his father by rafting down the river with Jim, a runaway slave. His book is a classic of American literature. His writing is famous partly for the lively and humorous characters, but also because Mark Twain tackled important racial and social issues.

Samuel Clemens first worked as a printer, but at the age of twenty-one he became a riverboat pilot. His adopted name, Mark Twain, comes from his experiences of life on the river. A steamboat hand testing the river's depth would call out 'mark twain' when the river was two fathoms deep, so telling the pilot where safe water was.

The American Civil War (1861 - 1865) stopped Mississippi River traffic. So Mark Twain moved to the state of Nevada, and began a new career as a journalist and writer. Today, the people of Hannibal still honour him. The Mark Twain Museum and the Mark Twain Boyhood Home show tourists more about the man and his work.

Above: Mark Twain, photographed in 1890. He often wore a white suit, like this one.

NATURE *The Big Muddy*

Twenty-nine kilometres north of the city of St Louis, two of the world's longest rivers - the Missouri and the Mississippi - come together.

The Missouri River is 3,725 kilometres long, so it is only fifty-five kilometres shorter than the Mississippi. It is the Mississippi's longest tributary, and it makes the Missouri-Mississippi river system the third longest in the world. (Only the Nile and the Amazon are longer.)

The Missouri drainage basin is enormous - about one-sixth of the entire landmass of the United States. This river contributes about twenty per cent of the Mississippi's total water flow. Here, at the confluence of the two rivers, you can see that happening right in front of you.

The Mississippi River takes on some of the Missouri River's personality, too. The Missouri is nicknamed the 'Big Muddy' because of its colour. The clear water of the Mississippi also becomes muddy when the Missouri's sediment - drained from agricultural land upstream - joins it.

Below: This aerial photograph shows exactly what happens when the clear water of the Mississippi River meets the muddy water of the Missouri River.

🐇 NATURE *Bursting the banks*

The Mississippi may seem to have been tamed by human actions, but nature has a habit of fighting back. During the twentieth century, regular flooding burst its banks several times.

The last 'big one' was in the summer of 1993. From April and throughout the summer, record levels of rain fell across the northern part of the drainage basin. Thunderstorms in June and July brought the heaviest rainfall for over a hundred years. As water drained off the land into the Mississippi and its tributaries, the river rose and broke its banks, and flooded on to the surrounding land.

Above: This photograph was taken in Clarkesville, Missouri, during the 1993 floods. The floodwaters are lapping up against the sandbags which protect Cooper's grocery store.

The impact of this was devastating. The Mississippi was closed to river traffic for two months, and vast areas along the Missouri and the Mississippi were affected. Property and crops were ruined, more than 70,000 people had to evacuate their homes, forty-eight people died, and US $12 billion of damage was left behind. Some areas recovered, but others did not. The town of Valmeyer in Illinois, for example, was abandoned after the disaster, and townspeople rebuilt on higher ground.

Hang on tightly as we travel on a fishing boat through St Louis to the choppy confluence of the Mississippi and the Ohio rivers.

Hannibal
Illinois River
ILLINOIS
Missouri River
Granite City
ST. LOUIS
Kaskaskia River
Valmeyer
MISSOURI
Cape Girardeau
Ohio River
2
Cairo
1
km 0   100
miles 0   50
New Madrid

3.The Middle Section

AS WE ENTER THE MIDDLE REACHES of the Mississippi we pass through the city of St Louis; the 'gateway to the west'. Two hundred years after explorers headed west into the unknown, the region still buzzes with activity. As we continue our journey downstream we will see one of the busiest ports in the country, some areas of outstanding natural beauty, and the confluence with the giant Ohio River.

Below: The Gateway Arch in St Louis, in the state of Missouri.
Right: This engraving of St Louis was made in 1830, when the town was truly a 'gateway' to the unexplored west.

📖 HISTORY *The Gateway Arch*

In 1804, under orders from President Thomas Jefferson, two explorers called Lewis and Clark led an expedition west from St Louis to search for the Pacific Ocean. When they returned to the city two and a half years later, after having travelled nearly 13,000 kilometres, St Louis gave them a tremendous welcome! The city became the entrance to the vast lands to the west, between the Mississippi and the Pacific.

As we journey through St Louis we are met by a wonderful sight, built as a monument to the pioneers who opened new areas of the country for settlement and trade. The gleaming, stainless steel Gateway Arch sits proudly on the riverbank, nearly 190 metres tall. (The foundations are a staggering eighteen metres deep.) If we take the four-minute ride to the top, we can see spectacular views of the city and the Mississippi. If you feel the building move, don't worry. The building is designed to sway two and a half centimetres in a thirty-two kilometres an hour wind, and nearly half a metre in an earthquake!

💲 ECONOMY *Floodwalls & levees*

St Louis bore the worst of the 1993 floods. On 17 July of that year, the volume of water passing the Gateway Arch jumped from the normal 4.7 million litres per second to a staggering 23.6 million litres per second! The flood peaked at nearly fifteen metres,

Above: A levee, broken by the force of water during the 1993 floods.

eleven metres higher than the usual level of the Mississippi River.

The city was protected by the massive floodwall and levees we see around us. These were constructed for the city by the United States government, after the catastrophic floods of 1927. In fact, the Mississippi River is 'walled in' by levees from Cape Girardeau to the sea.

The levees protect the immediate area, but the river is unable to meander and the floodwater cannot slowly spill on to the floodplain. The channelled water flows more quickly, and that puts stress on the levees further downstream. This, in turn, increases the risk of flooding in towns that are not fully protected, such as Valmeyer, mentioned on page 21.

$ ECONOMY A *transport centre*

St Louis, in the state of Missouri, was just a trading post for furs in the late eighteenth century. Its location, however, helped the city to become a key transportation centre. With the opening up of the west and the discovery of gold in California in 1849, St Louis was a major preparation point for people heading west in search of employment, wealth, and opportunity.

River traffic grew rapidly, and at one time as many as 170 steamboats could be seen lined up on the waterfront. When the Civil War ended in 1865, river transport had to compete with an expanding railroad network. The railroads ended the 'golden age' of steamboats. Trains were safer and more reliable than steamboats, and did not have to cope with the river freezing over in the winter!

Above: A line of paddle steamers stretches along St Louis' dock in this 1909 photograph. You can see the steam from the engines on several boats, as they prepare to leave. The route names are clear on the first two steamers

Today, although St Louis has one of the largest railway centres in the United States, river transport still thrives. Tows have replaced the steamboats, and the construction of locks and dams helped St Louis to become the second largest port on the inland waterway system.

The waterway system extends more than 110 kilometres along both banks of three rivers: the Missouri, the Kaskaskia, and the Mississippi. In 1998 the waterway handled nearly thirty-two million tons of goods. Winters can be cold in St Louis but they are not severe, so St Louis holds the title of the most northern ice-free port on the river.

PEOPLE *Town & country*

People who live and work in the countryside often have very different lifestyles to those based in towns and cities. Mississippi County MAP REF: 1 in the rural southeastern part of the state of Missouri is bounded on the north, east, and south by the Mississippi River. Poverty is higher and incomes are lower here than in the city of St Louis, and many people are leaving rural farming communities. During the 1990s the population of Mississippi County fell by seven per cent. People moved away to look for jobs, a better way of life, and improved living conditions.

Do people in urban areas have a better standard of life? Some people don't think so. In 1950 the population of St Louis city was more than 850,000. But over the next fifty years it fell dramatically, as people moved to the surrounding suburban districts. Now the city population is less than 350,000.

Below: You can see the Gateway Arch through the broken glass of these abandoned buildings in St Louis.
Bottom: Rural communities like this one in Mississippi County face an uncertain future.

NATURE *Wildlife & habitats*

The Mississippi is home to hundreds of species of plants, animals, birds, fish, and insects. More than 240 species of fish inhabit the river's water network, and 118 of these can be found between St Paul and Cairo! Forty per cent of North America's ducks, geese, swan and wading bird species use the river as a migration route. They breed in the north, and then travel down the river to spend winter in the milder southern climate.

As we go south we might see a Monarch butterfly hitch a ride on our boat, or even spot a bald eagle in the sky.

Any change to a river system will affect the surrounding environment, and the river's flow. The construction of locks and dams, the draining of wetlands, and the increase in shipping activities have all had such effects. Poor water quality, sedimentation, and loss of habitat are limiting the Mississippi's ability to support life. The peregrine falcon, the Higgins' Eye pearly mussel and the Iowa Pleistocene snail have all declined to near extinction. Yet there are some positive signs, too. Conservation organisations work to protect and monitor the river environment from the threats of pollution and over-exploitation.

A bald eagle, the symbol of the United States of America.

Above: The Ohio River, at the top of the
photograph, joins the Mississippi River
at the city of Cairo, in the state of Illinois.

Wildlife can often adapt to change. Walleye
fish, for example, like to shelter behind the
wingwalls that control the river flow in the
lower reaches of the river.

 NATURE *The Ohio River*

At Cairo, in the state of Illinois, we reach
the confluence of the muddy Mississippi
and the clear Ohio River. MAP REF: 2
The Ohio River and its own tributary, the
Tennessee River, contribute between them
an enormous sixty-two per cent of the
Mississippi's water. Much of this drains
from the Appalachian mountain range
to the east.

The 1993 floods centred on areas north
of Cairo. But it is more usual for the great
floods to occur beyond Cairo, in the lower
reaches of the Mississippi. Such floods are
often caused by snowmelt in the spring
thaw, and by the heavy rainfall that occurs
between January and May in the
Appalachian mountains.

Make sure you have your ticket to board
the Natchez and travel in style down the
lower reaches of the Mississippi.

4. The Lower Section

RELAX AND ENJOY THE SPLENDID old world charm of our steamboat, as we cruise from the confluence of the Ohio River to the city of Memphis. This steamboat journey recreates a part of American history. We will not stop to pick up furniture or deliver mail, as they did in the past. But we do see the tremendous floodplains and meanders, and experience the excitements of Memphis.

📖 **HISTORY** *Steamboat glory*

When you think of the Mississippi, you think of paddle steamers! They used to be the most important way of moving people, goods, and mail around America. The first steamer, the 'New Orleans', began operating in 1811, and steamboats brought wealth and development to the many settlements that sprang up along the river. The boat crews competed with each other, because the faster a boat was, the more passengers and businesses it would attract.

Below: This modern paddle steamer, named after the original 19th century Natchez, takes tourists on pleasure cruises.

Above: This old engraving shows the 1870 race between the 'Robert E Lee' and the 'Natchez'.

The most famous race was between the 'Robert E. Lee' and the 'Natchez', on 30 June 1870. Thousands of people watched, and an amazing US $2 million was bet on the outcome! The two boats set off from New Orleans to St Louis and after travelling the 1,200 kilometres of water in just three days, eighteen hours and fourteen minutes, the 'Robert E. Lee' claimed victory. (Her crew had removed all the windows, beds and other heavy objects to make their boat much lighter!)

The most famous steamboats were the tourist boats and casinos that provided cruises for wealthy Americans. These days, steamboats like ours still take tourists on cruises. The sense of history and the relaxing pace of the steamers are a popular escape from the fast-paced modern world.

NATURE *Shaking the foundations*

On 16 December 1811, this area experienced one of the most violent earthquakes in the history of America. When the earthquake struck, cracks in the ground opened and buildings up to 400 kilometres away were damaged. Even the church bells in Boston rang, 1,600 kilometres away! When the crew of the 'New Orleans' steamboat woke, the island to which they had moored near the town of New Madrid had disappeared into the river.

That earthquake registered eight on the Richter Scale. Scientists believe that a similar earthquake may strike within the next fifty years. If it does, the impact could be devastating because so many new towns and cities have sprung up here since 1811. A program has been introduced to help people survive earthquakes. New buildings are built to withstand them, and schools teach children what to do if an earthquake should strike.

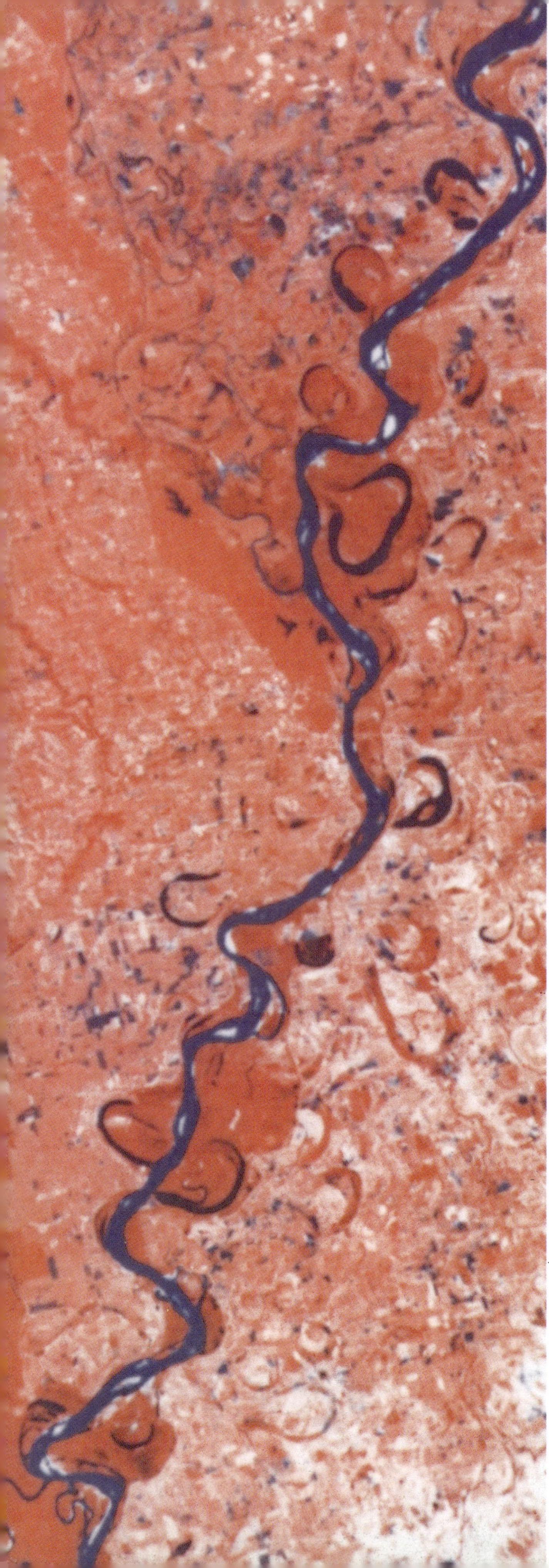

 NATURE *Winding downstream*

Our steamboat has to navigate several bends in this stretch of the river. It sometimes seems as if we are going back on ourselves! These bends are called meanders, and change their shape and position as they move slowly downstream towards the delta.

When water travels around a meander, the water on the outside moves faster than that on the inside. This extra force of the water means that the outside bank and river bed are eroded. The sediment is carried downstream, and deposited on the inside of the river bends, where the water moves more slowly. Over time, small beaches may form on the inside of a meander. Continued deposits of sediment can eventually cut the meander off from the main river. This forms a feature called an oxbow lake.

After the flood of 1927, the American Corps of Engineers cut channels through many meanders to reduce the risk of floods. This also reduced distances for river traffic. By the 1940s, about 240 kilometres had been cut from the original length!

At one time, the Mississippi River formed the border between the state of Mississippi on the east, and the states of Arkansas and Louisiana on the west. Changes in its course, however, mean that the state borders no longer follow the exact path of the river.

Left: A photograph taken by a NASA satellite of the Mississippi River and its floodplain, in the states of Arkansas and Mississippi. You can see meanders and oxbow lakes forming on both sides of the river. The photograph was taken in 1972, so the river's exact path will be different by now.

As we look out from the top deck of the steamboat, we can see flat land stretching away from the river. This is not the prairie we saw in the middle section, but a vast floodplain. This part of the river, which can be up to 1,600 metres wide, is slower than before and the descent is becoming gentler. When it is in flood, the river spills over this flat area of land, leaving a deposit of sediment when the floodwaters subside.

The combination of nutrient-rich sediment and flat land creates ideal farming conditions. Agriculture is a leading industry here. The state of Tennessee, for example, has about 80,000 farms. These generate more than US $2.4 billion worth of produce every year.

Left: Most farm produce is sold in massive quantities to supermarkets, or for export. But this Mississippi farmer with a small holding of agricultural land sells his vegetables locally, from a roadside stall.

Below: A levee (with a road on top of it) runs between the Mississippi on the left, and farmland on the right. But it is not high enough to stop the river flooding the land.

📖 HISTORY *Memphis, Tennessee*

Just before we enter the state of Mississippi we reach Memphis, the largest city in Tennessee. Built on bluffs above the river, Memphis was named after a town in Egypt, on the river Nile.

Memphis, Tennessee has a long and interesting history. The Chickasaw Native Americans called it Chisca, and farmed its surrounding plains. The Chickasaw lost control of the area. But Memphis still celebrates their culture in a museum where we can learn more about Native American history, and see a reconstruction of a traditional Chickasaw village.

Above: The blue glass Pyramid Arena in Memphis is thirty-two storeys high. It is an entertainment and sports centre, and home to the local basketball team, the Memphis Grizzlies.

We can still see old warehouses along the river, from when the city was an important cotton port and naval shipyard. There are also modern office buildings and new business centres. Many tourists visit Memphis to see the Mud Island Museum, which tells the history of the Mississippi. The National Civil Rights Museum is also in Memphis. It honours the civil rights leader, the Reverend Dr Martin Luther King, who was assassinated here in 1968.

Right: The King Bees blues band playing in B.B. King's club on Beale Street.

Elvis Presley sold more than a billion records, more than anyone else in the history of the music industry.

PEOPLE *Blues & Rock*

Memphis is most famous for its music, so we must visit Beale Street, the home of the Blues. The city has had strong musical traditions since the nineteenth century. W.C. Handy moved here from Alabama in 1902, and played in the bars of Beale Street. His musical style was influenced by the musical traditions from Africa, brought to America by black slaves. This music developed into what we now call the Blues.

Memphis is also the birthplace of Rock 'n'Roll. This music style was developed in the 1950s, as a faster version of Blues. It soon appealed to young people all around the world, and made Memphis' greatest star, Elvis Presley, world famous. After Elvis died in 1977 his home, Graceland, MAP REF: 1 was turned into a museum. Hundreds of thousands of people visit Graceland every year, to remember and celebrate the life and music of the King of Rock'n'Roll.

📖 HISTORY *Slavery & cotton*

The flat ground, rich soil and warm climate of this area make it perfect for growing cotton. In 1793, a machine called a cotton gin was invented, that separated the seed from the cotton head. The cotton gin speeded up production, and made cotton a much more profitable crop.

Demand for cotton in the textile mills of the northern states and Great Britain was very high. Cotton soon became the United States' leading export. Steamboats transported large quantities of the crop up and down the Mississippi River.

Above: Black field hands harvesting cotton by hand in 1880, and a modern harvesting machine.

Cotton was picked by hand, and the plantation owners used African slaves to do this work. Slaves had no human rights at all. They were unpaid, and forced to live and work in terrible conditions.

Slavery ended in 1865, after the Civil War. By then, about four million African-Americans lived in the southern United States. Slaves had been forbidden to learn to read or write, and they had no land, homes or jobs. Their lives were still very hard.

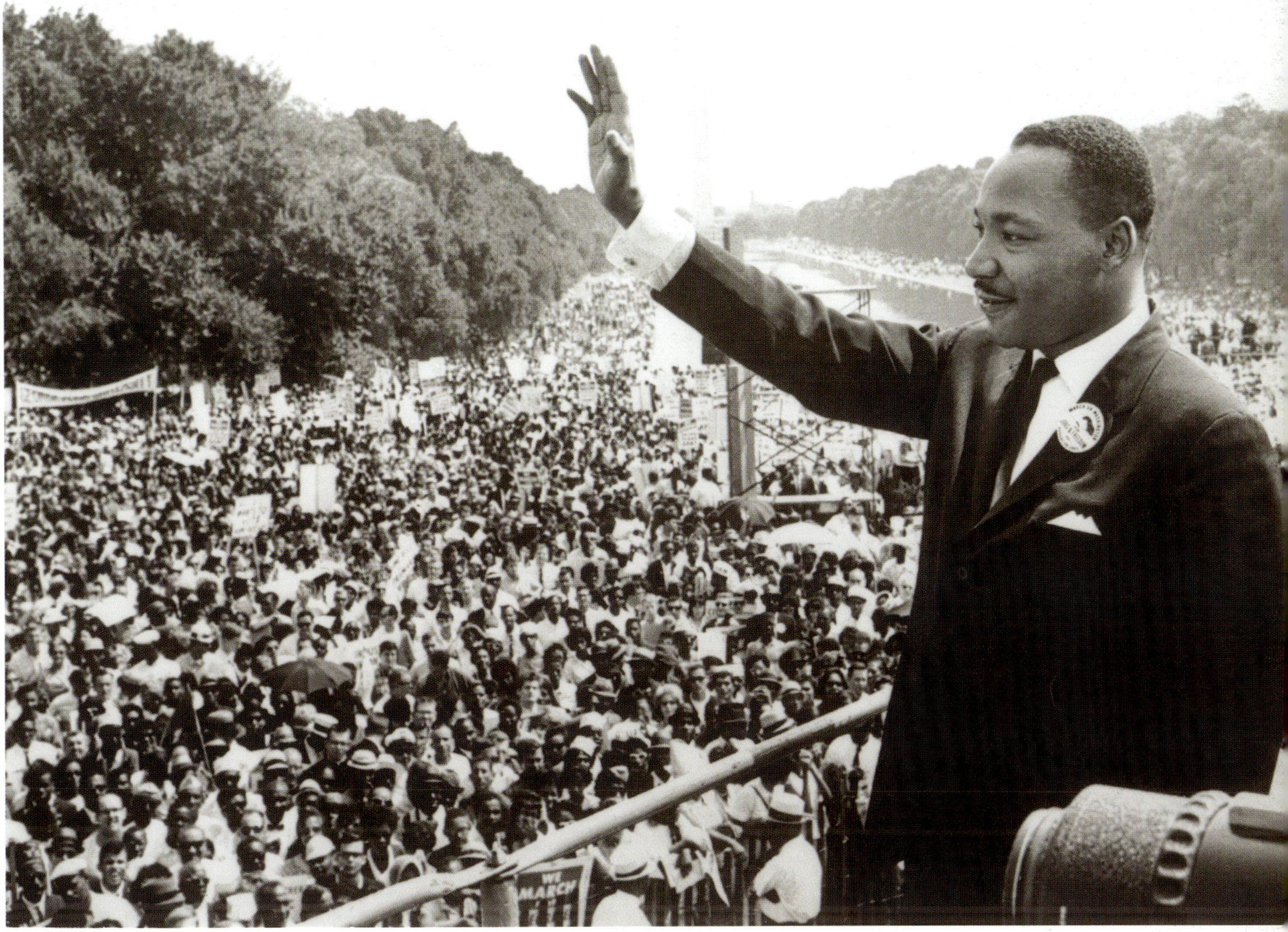

Above: In 1963, the Reverend Dr. Martin Luther King led a civil rights march to Washington, the capital of the USA. Tens of thousands of black and white Americans joined the march.

PEOPLE *Civil rights*

By the middle of the twentieth century, civil rights campaigns, especially those led by Martin Luther King, had helped gain equal rights for everyone. Since then, African-Americans have had a greater role in US politics, and many have been elected to local and national positions. But racial tensions, and inequalities still exist - especially in southern states such as Arkansas and Mississippi.

In an attempt to deal with the terrible memories and abuses of slavery, a new campaign has begun. Led by a group of important lawyers and lecturers, the campaign demands that the United States government should pay compensation to the families of former slaves.

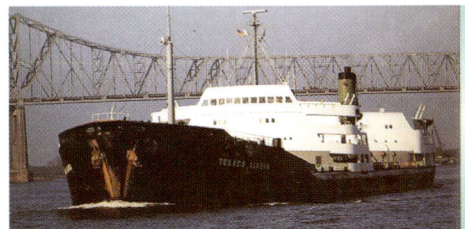

As we pass into the delta we leave the luxury of our paddle steamer. A tanker will pick us up at Baton Rouge. We can take its cargo of oil to the Gulf of Mexico - and beyond.

Below: An 1832 painting of the military barracks in Baton Rouge. You can see a red cypress tree on the left - the 'baton rouge', or 'red stick', of the city's name.

5. The Delta

WE HAVE REACHED THE DELTA – the final section of the river. Here, we see very different landscapes. The vast wetlands, natural levees and channels of one of the world's largest deltas replace the valleys and bluffs we have travelled through. Oil and gas pipelines crisscross the area as we make our way to the fishing grounds of the Gulf of Mexico, and to the oceans beyond.

📖 HISTORY *Baton Rouge*

Many different peoples - Native Americans, French, English, Spanish, Italians, and Africans - have settled in this region. They have all shaped the colourful history of Baton Rouge, the capital of the state of Louisiana.

In French, 'baton rouge' means 'red stick', and the city's name comes from a red cypress tree that grew here. It marked the line between the hunting grounds of the Houma and Bayou Goula Native Americans, to whom the area originally belonged. In 1719, the French built a fort to provide support for traders who were travelling upstream from New Orleans. During the next century the British, the Spanish, and

Above: Oil refineries line the Mississippi in Baton Rouge. Exxon, a petro-chemical corporation, is a major employer here.

the French each controlled Baton Rouge for a time. It finally became part of the United States in 1810.

Baton Rouge has always been a true river settlement, and the Mississippi offers trade opportunities as well as transportation. The city has played a central role in different aspects of the region's history. It has been a port and commercial centre for sugar cane and cotton plantations, a military site during the Civil War, and most recently, a national centre for the oil and gas industry and river transport businesses.

$ ECONOMY *Gate to the Gulf*

Baton Rouge is 370 kilometres from the Gulf of Mexico, and the furthest point upstream that big ocean-going ships can reach. From here, only tows can take goods further north along the shallower reaches of the Mississippi.

Baton Rouge's port - the fourth largest in the United States and the eighteenth largest in the world - bustles with ships and tankers. From here, steel, oil, gas, soybeans, sugar cane and other goods are shipped into the Gulf of Mexico, past the Caribbean Islands and on to the Atlantic or Pacific oceans.

More than 1,400 billion litres of water flow past the city every day. This is ideal for manufacturers needing large amounts of water for their businesses. But with the water, comes sediment. To stop the channel becoming too shallow for the vast ocean-going vessels, a dredge constantly travels along it, scooping up sediment.

NATURE *Ooze & sediment*

Viewed from above, deltas often look like birds' feet - or like the fourth letter of the Greek alphabet, Δ, which is called 'delta'. The Mississippi delta has formed where the river, with all its energy and sediment, meets the relatively calm Gulf of Mexico. The Mississippi slows, and as it does so it deposits sediment at a faster rate than the sea can remove it.

Over time the sediment gradually builds up, and extends out. When the river channels become blocked with sediment, the water tries to find another route to the open sea - and the channels overflow.

The flooding of the land and the sediment left behind make the land very fertile. The warm climate and continuous supply of water make this a great place to grow crops such as sugar cane and rice.

Migratory birds love the nutrient-rich waters of the delta region, and they feed on some of the 183 species of fish that live in these waters. Black bears and Florida panthers live in the delta forests - so if you decide to head ashore, then stay alert!

Below: The channels, streams and lakes of the delta spread out as far as the eye can see.

The changing delta

The Mississippi delta is one of the oldest in the world. Until about one hundred years ago it was still growing, month-by-month, year-by-year. Over the last century, however, the area where we are travelling has been both sinking and shrinking. The coastline is moving backwards by up to twenty-five metres every year. That might not sound very much, but it means that one acre of land is lost every twenty-four minutes!

Land is often lost in delta environments as a result of natural processes, but changes in the Mississippi delta are not entirely natural. The construction of canals and levees, the dredging of channels, and the building of flood defences upstream have all altered the river's flow.

Most importantly, the Mississippi River now carries less sediment - and sediment is the lifeline of the delta. Environmental campaigners believe that if action is not taken to reduce sediment loss (for example, by cutting back on dredging) then delta habitats could be lost. Campaigners also point out that changes in the delta could harm the fishing, oil and gas industries.

Below: Levees protect the land, but stop the natural cycle of flooding that the delta needs. It's a difficult balance to maintain.

$ ECONOMY *Oil & gas*

The discovery of oil and gas in Louisiana state and the Gulf of Mexico in 1901 has changed the landscape of the delta region. The tanker on which we are travelling carries oil extracted by some 22,000 wells from deep under the delta. We can see some of the wells around us as we travel.

From the wells, the oil is piped to one of fifteen refineries in Louisiana, where it is cleaned and then separated into different products. You may think of oil as just a fuel for transport or energy production, but it is also used as a raw material in the manufacture of computer parts, plastics, VCRs, CDs and medicine.

Around 75,000 people were employed in this oil and gas industry in 1999, but many more are employed by the business and industries that provide goods and services to the oil and gas workers and their families.

Above: An oil rig in the marshy delta land along the coast of Louisiana.

NATURE *Environmental threats*

Natural gas and oil are used by hundreds of millions of people around the world but finding, producing and refining these products can damage the environment.

More than 45,000 kilometres of pipeline crisscross the delta as a visible scar on the environment. Less visible are the dangerous chemical wastes pumped into the delta by the surrounding industries and agriculture. Pollution from these wastes combined with habitat loss due to human activity threaten several species of bird, reptile, fish and shellfish.

Delta wildlife is also threatened by the introduction of species that are not native to the area. The zebra mussel, for example, was introduced by accident in the northern

Great Lakes, and quickly spread downriver. Now, it has caused the native shellfish populations to collapse. Ornamental water hyacinths have also entered the delta, where they choke waterways and deprive local plants of light and oxygen.

Some action has been taken to clean up the area, and the Oil Pollution Act of 1990 has helped. Pollution in the state of Louisiana fell by eighty-one per cent between 1987 and 1994, and reserves have been set up to protect wildlife. In 1935, for example, the Delta National Wildlife Refuge MAP REF: 1 was created in southeastern Louisiana. This protects a large area of natural habitat, and gives people the chance to visit the marshland and see its wildlife.

Left: Cutting out water hyacinths from the river.
Below: The Jean Lafitte National Park in the state of Louisiana. Here, an old logging canal meets a natural canal in the bayou (the local name for a marshy offshoot of a river).

Above: The Mississippi flows like a great curving snake, through the heart of New Orleans.

✋ PEOPLE *The Big Easy*

Welcome to the Big Easy - the local name for the city of New Orleans! This city has boomed since it was founded in 1718, despite problems like hurricanes, mosquito-borne diseases such as malaria, and floods. It now contains the second largest port in the country.

New Orleans is also known as the Crescent City, because of the way the Mississippi River curves around the city's central district. In fact, because the city lies between the river and Lake Pontchartrain, different parts of New Orleans are linked with a system of bridges. One of these, the Pontchartrain Causeway, MAP REF: 2 is thirty-eight kilometres long. That makes it the longest over-water highway in the world.

New Orleans is home to nearly 500,000 people, of whom sixty-two per cent are African-American, thirty-five per cent are white, and three per cent are Hispanic.

The city provides a fascinating mix of music, food, and culture. Louis Armstrong, one of the most talented jazz musicians in history, was born here in 1901. In his early years he often played on boats that travelled on the Mississippi.

Louis Armstrong, the great jazz trumpeter.

New Orleans has a semi-tropical climate, and a relaxed atmosphere. These qualities have made it one of the most popular tourist cities in the United States. As they say here - 'Laissez les bons temps rouler' or 'Let the good times roll'!

✋ PEOPLE *Mardi Gras*

About a month before the Christian festival of Easter is another festival, called Mardi Gras - which means 'Fat Tuesday' in French. The New Orleans Mardi Gras has become one of the most spectacular events in the world, and over four million people travel there each year, to take part.

Parades with decorated floats and elaborate costumes, as well as music and

Above: Almost two thousand Mardi Gras parades have been held in New Orleans since 1857.

dance, are just the start of the fun. People often wear the official colours of the festival: purple, gold and green, which stand for justice, faith and power. Each parade has a theme, influenced by characters from children's stories, famous people, arts and literature, history, and even geography.

The enjoyment of partygoers during Mardi Gras is shared by local business owners. Nearly all the 30,000 hotel rooms in New Orleans are filled during the festival, and Mardi Gras earns the city over US $840 million each year!

🐇 NATURE · *The final destination*

From New Orleans we enter the Gulf of Mexico, which is like a long finger pointing up from the Atlantic Ocean. The Gulf, which covers about 1.5 million square kilometres, touches America to the north, Mexico to the south and west, and Cuba to the east. This stretch of sea is the final destination for the waters of the Mississippi, and every second about seventeen million litres of water drain into the Gulf. Tourists, many of whom come here to fish, support thousands of businesses and tens of thousands of jobs.

$ ECONOMY · *Looking for a bite*

Every year, more than twenty four million trips are made here by people holidaying in the Gulf of Mexico. Snapper, redfish, flounder, trout and pompano all await those with the patience and skill to catch a meal!

Recreational fishers are not the only people looking for a catch. About forty per cent of America's entire fish harvest comes from the Gulf of Mexico, and shrimps make up more than one half of the catch. Commercial and recreational fishing makes about US $2.8 billion each year.

Those who eat seafood, however, face growing dangers. High pollution levels mean that about half the shellfish-producing areas, and many oyster beds, can no longer be used. This has had an enormous impact on the fishing industry. Commercial fishers are forced either to stop work altogether, or to fish in other waters. Recreational fishers may also become less attracted to the area - and that will hurt the tourist industry.

Left: A Cajun fisherman in the Atchafalaya Basin - a swampy area of wetlands that flows into the Mississippi River.
Above right: A shrimp boat spreading its nets in the Gulf of Mexico.
Below right: American oysters, gathered for sale to seafood restaurants in New Orleans.

SO THERE IT IS: THE MIGHTY MISSISSIPPI. You have seen and experienced a river system that has helped to shape modern-day America. The Mississippi River is forever changing, offering new opportunities to its people and facing new threats to its future.

But one thing is certain. As the river's course and delta continue to change, and the danger of flooding and earthquakes remain, the Mississippi will never be far from the news. So be sure to watch out for new episodes in the river's story.

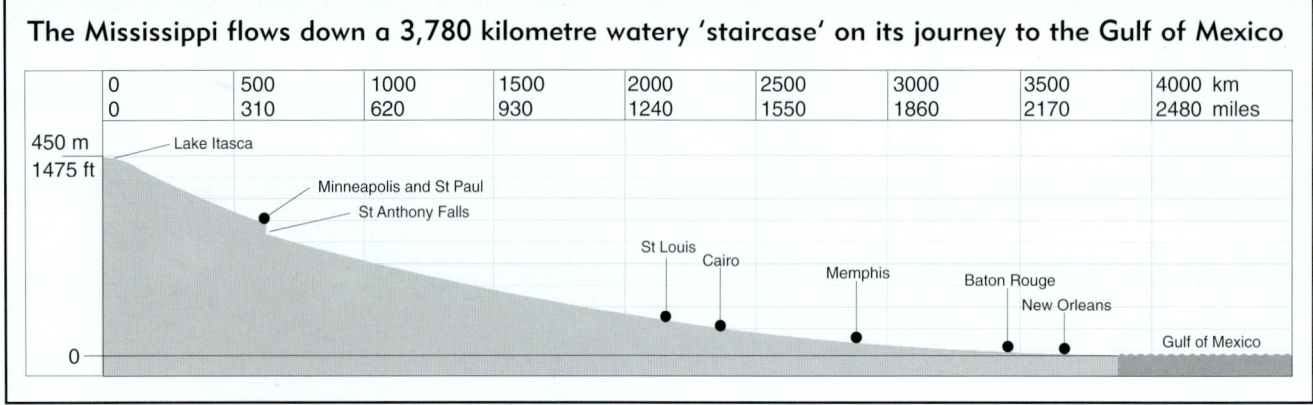

The Mississippi flows down a 3,780 kilometre watery 'staircase' on its journey to the Gulf of Mexico

| | 0 | 500 | 1000 | 1500 | 2000 | 2500 | 3000 | 3500 | 4000 km |
| | 0 | 310 | 620 | 930 | 1240 | 1550 | 1860 | 2170 | 2480 miles |

450 m
1475 ft — Lake Itasca

Minneapolis and St Paul
St Anthony Falls

St Louis
Cairo
Memphis
Baton Rouge
New Orleans
Gulf of Mexico

0

Further Information

American Rivers National Office,
1025 Vermont Avenue, N.W.
Suite 720,
Washington, DC 20005, USA
http://www.americanrivers.org

Friends of the Mississippi River,
46 East 4th Street, Suite 606,
St Paul MN, 55101-1112
USA
http://www.fmr.org

Mississippi River Parkway Commission,
PO Box 59159
Minnesota 55459
USA
http://www.mississippiriverinfo.com

Upper Mississippi River Conservation Committee,
4469 48th Ave. Court,
Rock Island,
Illinois 61201
USA
http://www.mississippi-river.com/umrcc

The Mark Twain House,
351 Farmington Avenue,
Hartford, CT 06105
USA
http://www.marktwainhouse.org

Books:

Earth in Danger: Rivers by Polly Goodman (Hodder Wayland, 2005)

Geography Fact Files: Rivers by Mandy Ross (Hodder Wayland, 2004)

Rivers in Action by Mary Green (Franklin Watts, 2003)

The Mississippi by Michael Pollard (Evans Brothers, 2003)

Themes in Geography: Rivers by Fred Martyn (Heinemann Library, 1996)

Glossary

Bank The side of a river.

Barge A long riverboat used to transport goods. Barges usually have no engines, and are moved by tows.

Bluff A steep cliff on the side of the river.

Cajun People of French-Canadian descent who moved to Louisiana in the 1800s.

Canal An artificial water channel, cut for navigation or irrigation.

Cereal Farm crops that produce grains such as wheat and maize.

Channel The passage through which a river flows.

Civil war A war fought between people in the same country. The American Civil War took place from 1861 to 1865, between the northern Union Army and the southern Confederate Army.

Confluence The place where two rivers meet.

Current The flow of water in a certain direction.

Dam A barrier that holds or diverts water.

Delta A geographical feature at the mouth of a river, formed by the build-up of sediment.

Descent A downward change in height.

Downstream Towards the mouth of a river.

Drainage basin The area of land that is drained by a river and its tributaries.

Dredge To clear or deepen a waterway or a port, by scooping or sucking up sediment.

Erosion The wearing away of land by natural forces such as running water, glaciers, wind or waves.

Flood When a river spills over its banks, on to land that is usually dry.

Floodplain The part of a river valley submerged during floods.

Habitat The home of animals and plants.

Hardwoods Wood from trees such as oak, elm, ebony and teak.

Headwater Water at the source of a river.

Hispanic Someone of Latin American or Spanish origin.

Levee A long, narrow bank that keeps the river within its channel. Levees may be natural or artificial barriers.

Lock An enclosed section of river, where the water level can be raised or lowered. This helps ships move up or down the river.

Lumber Timber sawn into planks.

Malaria A disease carried by mosquitoes.

Meander A large bend in a river.

Meltwater Water produced by the melting of snow and ice.

Migration Movement of animals or birds to take advantage of the changing seasons.

Ooze Soft mud found on the bottom of rivers.

Oxbow lake A small, arc-shaped lake that was once part of the former course of a river.

Plunge pool A hollow found at the base of a waterfall. It is caused by erosion.

Pollution Harmful waste released into the environment.

Population density The number of people living in a given area.

Port A place by water, used to load and unload ships.

Rapids Fast-moving stretches of water.

Reservation An area of land set aside to protect a natural habitat or a group of people.

Sediment Fine sand and earth that is moved and left by water, wind or ice.

Snowmelt Water that comes from melting snow.

Sod Another word for earth, or ground, when it is covered in grass.

Source The point at which a river begins.

Steamboat A boat driven by a steam engine. The engine turns large, circular paddlewheels, which move the boat.

Tanker A ship that carries oil or other liquids in large quantities.

Tow A towboat and its barges. Tows often push rather than pull, or tow barges along.

Tributary A stream or river that flows into another larger stream or river.

Upstream Towards the source of a river.

Vessel A ship or boat.

Waterfall A sudden fall of water over a steep drop.

Watershed The boundary between two river basins.

Wetland An area that is often wet or flooded.

Wingwalls Walls around a bridge that keep the river flowing smoothly.

Index